SAVVY!

THE YOUNG WOMAN'S GUIDE TO
CAREER SUCCESS

THORNE
CONNELLY
PUBLISHING

Library of Congress Cataloging-in-Publication data: in progress
ISBN: 978-0-692-20220-3

First edition.

SAVVY!

THE YOUNG WOMAN'S GUIDE TO CAREER SUCCESS

ALICE NAGLE
&
LUANNE TIERNEY

*In the spirit of passing advice from one generation to the next,
we'd like to thank our original mentors, our moms.
We appreciate your support and guidance—
even though you're not so savvy on digital devices!*

Contents

1
Set Career Goals

YOU are the CEO of your career. No one is going to spend more time thinking about your career than you. We're providing you with practical advice for the business world so you can fast track your career. First tip: set your goals.

Ready? Get started! Put all of your digital devices down and grab a piece of paper and your favorite pen and write them down. Why are we asking you to write them down? When you literally write them your brain registers them more deeply than when they are typed.

Most successful people are goal setters. Sara Blakely, founder of the multi-million-dollar company Spanx, had a goal at 27 of wanting her bottom to look better in white pants, according to an interview in *SUCCESS Magazine*. Sheryl Sandberg, Facebook COO and author of *Lean In: Women, Work, and the Will to Lead*, said, "My whole life has been an accumulation of obtainable goals." Andrea Sittig-Rolf, CEO of BlitzMasters, a corporate sales training firm, achieved her goal of becoming a successful entrepreneur through daily creative visualization: imagining her own success.

What are your goals? Self-reflection requires honesty. These are not your parents' goals or what you think is expected of you. Think of your future "selfie"!

As you imagine the future successful you, here are some questions to consider. It's ok if you don't have clear answers right away. Continue to ponder and reflect as you have more experiences and gain more self-awareness.

- What's my purpose? What are my gifts and what's important to me? What kind of work is interesting to me?

- In five years, what do I want to be doing?

- What are my career aspirations? Do I want to manage a team? Work internationally? Do I want to work in a big or small company? How far up the ladder do I want to go?

- What kind of work environment suits me? Do I prefer an open social environment or more solitude?

- What motivates me to do my best work? Money? Competition? Dreams of being a leader and increased responsibility? Recognition? Flexibility? The people I work for and with?

- What stresses me out?

- Where are the gaps between where I'm headed and where I am today? What experiences, knowledge, and skills do I need to bridge those gaps?

Some people find that sharing their goals helps them feel accountable. Choose a friend, a co-worker, a mentor, or someone you trust to check in with and keep you on track.

Over the years, Luanne has worked with Loraine, a strategic adviser who prompted Luanne to think about the position she wanted long term early on. At the time, Luanne was so busy surviving as a young working mom, it seemed there was no time to slow down and think of her aspirational career goals. Loraine's prompting forced Luanne to set aside the time to think about the questions we've spelled out for you. She decided to embrace a long-term career of becoming a visible marketing executive. As a result, she honestly evaluated what was missing in her skills that would take her to the next level—and she put an emphasis on developing her public speaking and communication skills. Finding that person who will have that conversation with you and cheer you on over time can be incredibly rewarding when setting and achieving your goals.

Taking little steps every day will add up over time. Think of the person who's never run a marathon and takes that on as a goal. She may start out walking, then running. Within a few months, if she's consistent with her training, she can run 26 miles.

Be flexible with your goals. As you have new experiences, especially early in your career, you'll learn more about what you want and what you don't, what you're good at, and what you're interested in. Your goals will change and evolve over time. Revise them. Make adjustments. Don't be passive in your career. Stay in the driver's seat, actively setting and redefining your goals.

Management Consultant Peter Drucker's SMART method for setting goals

Specific	Answer the basic questions of who, what, where, when, and why.
Measurable	Make your goals quantifiable so you can track progress.
Attainable	Set realistic goals—but push yourself.
Relevant	Establish goals that support your vision.
Time-bound	Set deadlines so you stay on track.

MY CAREER GOALS

2
Create a Personal Brand

EVERYONE has a brand. It's what you're known for. If you're just graduating from college, you've been affiliated with your major, GPA, sorority, or college. As you transition to work, your brand is about your professional reputation. It's bigger than your job title or the company you work for. It's how someone who knows you would describe you to someone who doesn't. In fact, it's how people who don't know you at all describe you to strangers.

"Regardless of age, regardless of position, regardless of the business we happen to be in, all of us need to understand the importance of branding," Tom Peters, an author on business management practices, said in a *Fast Company* article. "We are the CEOs of our own companies: Me, Inc. To be in business today, our most important job is to be head marketer for the brand called You."

As you start your career, clarify the impression you want to create about yourself in the minds of others. What are the three unique qualities, skills, and/or technologies you want to be known for? What differentiates you from your peers?

Here's a perfect example. Years ago, Alexis, who is in sales in Washington D.C., wrote down the words she wanted to be associated with: tenacious, polished executive, and executive presence. She consciously "exemplifies those words consistently and often." Clearly, it's working for her. She was promoted several times, from an associate to the top Account Manager position, in five years and has been recognized by her company as among the top 10% of sales people. You'll notice that even though she was at the start of her career, she called out executive presence.

"Executive presence is a heady combination of confidence, poise, and authenticity that convinces the rest of us we're in the presence of someone who's the real deal," explains Sylvia Ann Hewlett in her book *Executive Presence: The Missing Link Between Merit and Success.* "It's a measure of image: whether you signal to others that you have what it takes, that you're star material.'

"Managing your personal brand is almost a full time job unto itself, lest it be managed for you by people who don't hold your best interests at heart," Hewlett writes. "You've got to be proactive in asserting who you are, what you stand for, and how you'd like to be perceived."

As you think about your brand, here are important characteristics to consider:

- Claim your strengths. If you think that articulating your strengths and gifts is bragging, then you need to change your thinking. This isn't the time to be timid. Building a strong, positive brand is critical for exuding confidence and power. If you're not sure where your strengths lie, go online to the Gallup Strengths Center (www.gallupstrengthscenter.com) and take their assessment. It's based on 50 years of research and will provide a comprehensive report of your unique set of strengths. There's a fee—but sometimes the company you work for will pick up the tab as a professional development expense.

- Make your brand distinctive; differentiate yourself from your peers. For example: "polished and confident communicator" is more specific than "good writer."

- Use verbs rather than nouns. For example: "solves problems through proactive ideas and great collaboration skills" is better than "good problem solver."

- Pick powerful words. Strategic, leadership, proactive rather than weaker words, such as hard-working, multitasker, supportive.

- Make your brand aspirational; it's about your future. As you think about the next steps in your career, how do you want to be seen and what skills will be required? Leading teams, initiating creative solutions to help your company grow, and demonstrating executive presence are examples of aspirational brand attributes.

If you're not clear on your brand yet, it may become apparent over time as your career unfolds. By the time Alice was in her 30s, she realized she was developing a pattern of success when working with senior business leaders. In her 40s, she spent the majority of her workdays developing communications strategies for and being a trusted adviser to executive vice presidents and CEOs. The mix of being a communications expert, seeing the big picture, remaining calm in high stress situations, and delivering results became her hallmark when working with executives.

Your brand is connected to everything you show the world. Think of a "brand molecule" with a cluster of efforts connected to the core of the molecule: your brand. It's your online presence, how you dress, how you decorate your cubicle or office, how you communicate, and how you show up at work. You also have to pay attention to what hurts your brand: typos in your emails, inaccuracies in a report you produce, and lack of follow-through. Effective branding is about sending a strong and consistent message.

Brand expert William Arruda, who wrote *Career Distinction: Stand Out by Building Your Brand* and *Ditch, Dare, Do: 3D Personal Branding for Executives* and has helped both Alice and Luanne with their personal brands, says developing your brand is an intelligent move for the savvy professional. Luanne applied William's advice when she was a director at Cisco and found it made a significant impact to her career. She took the time to identify her three brand attributes at the time: marketing innovator, mentor to other women, social media expert.She noticed it made it easier to be identified and recognized throughout the company and industry.

"As a professional, your reputation is your most valuable career asset," Arruda says. "Whether you're climbing the ladder at your current company or seeking a new job, in today's fast-paced work environment you must proactively and continuously position yourself for success. Your credibility, visibility, personality, and personal style all make up your brand. Build and nurture your personal brand and you'll make yourself a must-have, can't fail professional—and you'll do it without having to be someone you're not."

A compelling brand is developed over time—often, many years—and you are responsible for making that happen. It takes conscious effort. The upside is that once people know who you are and what you stand for, it's more likely they will consider you for projects, jobs, promotions, and interesting opportunities.

PERSON	BRAND ATTRIBUTE	BRAND ATTRIBUTE	BRAND ATTRIBUTE
Marissa Mayer, CEO of Yahoo!	Executive known for technology market transitions and innovation	Exceptional design (technology, fashion)	One of the youngest and most powerful women in business
Lauren Bush, co-founder and CEO of FEED Projects	High fashion model	Philanthropist: feeding children around the world	Change agent in the conscious consumer movement
Clara Shih, author and CEO, Hearsay Social	Thought leader on social media	Connecting business and technology	Quiet leadership style
Lauren Conrad, TV personality, fashion designer, and author	Trendsetter and fashion advisor to young women	Classic, understated style; classy vs. trashy	Lovely, chic lifestyle
Tiffani Bova, Distinguished Analyst, Gartner, named one of the most powerful and influential women in California by the Diversity Council, 2014.	Technology thought leader and straight talking technologist	Boosting sales performance and renewing competitiveness through sales innovation	Building your "tribe" (your close professional network) as a multiplier effect for thought leadership
Jennifer Lawrence, actress	Actress with range, known for diversity of roles	The imperfect actress and proud of it	Down to earth with a good head on her shoulders

Are you with us? Defining and managing your brand is really important! Get that piece of paper out where you wrote down your goals—or use the space below—and write the three things you stand for. Be bold and aspirational. Be creative. Have fun with this!

✒ *THREE THINGS I WANT TO BE KNOWN FOR.*

3

Manage Your Online Presence

WE know you've been texting since you were two and can multitask on every digital platform while pumping gas, but let's continue the conversation about your brand.

"Your reputation online matters, which in the new business world is pretty much the game," says Gary Vaynerchuk in *Jab, Jab, Jab, Right Hook: How to Tell Your Story in a Noisy Social World*.

Here are three great reasons to invest time in building out your professional online brand. First, it's a vital way to amplify the brand you defined for yourself. Second, it's a global job-networking machine. In Katherine Schwarzenegger's book *I Just Graduated . . . Now What?*, she writes, "These days, lots of employers search the hundreds of millions of members on LinkedIn based on skill set, experience, school affiliations, connections, and relationships. If you are not searchable by these traits and factors, no one can find you." Lastly, it's a great source for finding people and information relevant to you.

Here are four strategies for building and enhancing your online brand:

1. Assess your online presence. Google yourself. Does the search bring up images and words that are in line with your brand? Are you connected to ideas and words that support your brand and what you want to be known for?

2. Claim your online name. Use namecheck.com to see if the online domain name you'd like to use, whether it's your own name or a tagline, is taken or available. It's a great way to protect your name and to safeguard it if you start a business in the future.

3. Create a Social Media Profile. Of the three online tools (LinkedIn, Twitter, and Google+), LinkedIn is the most important, professionally. Spend time making sure it projects your brand.

LinkedIn "must haves"

Profile must be simple, descriptive, and easy to read.

- Write in the first person ("I" rather than "she") and use headlines rather than full sentences.

- Invest in a high-quality professional image. We emphasize the word "professional"; no cropped family photos and/or low-cut blouses. If you can afford it, spending $100 on a professional headshot is a great investment in your career. If possible, update your photo every year. Your LinkedIn profile is 40% more likely to be clicked on if it contains a photo, according to theladders.com job search engine.

- Use Search Engine Optimization (SEO) words and terms that you want to be associated with and that tie to your career goals. This will bring you to the top of Google and LinkedIn searches. Examples: Communications Expertise, Digital/CRM Skills, Strong Program Management Skills.

- Make the most of the valuable real estate under your name. Once again, think in terms of "headlines" that will attract attention. Your job title is not a headline!

- Be brief and demonstrate impact in your summary, skills, and expertise. Your summary describes the value you bring. List skills and expertise that are important to your customers and clients. Make your results quantifiable whenever possible. Data and industry statistics add credibility.

- Take advantage of LinkedIn "Professional Portfolio" to demonstrate your accomplishments. Share presentations, videos, links, and PDFs. One of the hottest trends is to post a short 15-20 second video in your portfolio.

4. Keep your online brand clean. Now that you're in the work world, you've got a new online audience. It might be your boss, your customers, or the HR department. Remember: everyone Googles you before they meet with you. Think of your online photos and the photos you're tagged in as a public billboard for your new professional brand. Be thoughtful about what you post. We don't want to lecture, but people lose job offers and get fired for not paying attention to this. Prioritize your online brand—and keep in mind these simple suggestions:

- Be careful what you say online about other people, companies, and politically charged topics.

- Don't post photos of yourself with alcohol or in inappropriate settings or inappropriate clothing.

- Don't "sip and send." Big mistakes can happen when our judgment is clouded by alcohol.

- Monitor your brand for unflattering photos and mentions of you with services like Google Alerts, reputation.com, and brandyourself.com.

4

Make Your Boss Successful

EVERYBODY'S got a boss. Even a CEO reports to the Board of Directors. Your boss has power over your performance reviews, salary and bonus decisions, and your advancement. It's in your best interest to make this relationship work. Success at work is not just about doing your own job well; it's about helping your boss do his or her job well, too. Making your boss successful will help you get ahead!

Understand how your boss operates. We've found that you can get the relationship off to a good start by asking some of these basic questions in one of your initial meetings:

- What does success look like for me in this role?

- How do you prefer that I communicate with you? Voicemail? Email? Instant messaging? Informally stop by your office?

- How do you like to get updates (email, text, voicemail) and how often?

- How in the loop do you want to be? (For example,

do you want to be copied on emails and included in important meetings?)

- How do you want me to communicate with you when I'm having a work problem? How important is it that I come to you first in resolving problems?

- How involved do you want to be in approving my projects?

- What are your top priorities? How can I help you achieve them?

- How will I be measured?

- What are the characteristics of your best employees?

- How often do you want to meet? (Most managers will have regular one-on-one meetings with their employees.)

We want to emphasize that it's *your* responsibility to make this relationship work.

One young woman we interviewed, Sadie, came into her first job in biotech sales in San Francisco with the confidence that comes from being a great student with a strong GPA. She admits she had a bit of an attitude when she started her job—and didn't realize her boss took it as arrogant. A year into her role, she figured out that she needed to understand what her boss was trying to accomplish and have a more supportive approach. Once she aligned with her boss, she was surprised how things changed. Her boss spent more time talking to her and became interested in the value Sadie was providing to the company. Soon, she was promoted to regional manager.

If you don't pay attention, you could have avoidable problems with your boss. When Alice was 25, for example, she was working in a communications role at AT&T. She got an inquiry from a reporter that was out of the scope of her role. She went to the media relations district manager to ask for advice. Unbeknownst to her, her boss watched her go into his peer's office for help—and immediately reprimanded her by saying, "In the future go through me, not around me." It was an innocent mistake, but, clearly, Alice hit a nerve with her boss, who was "old school" about reporting lines.

When you meet with your boss, be prepared. Bring a list of topics to discuss, whether they're work updates or a summary of your accomplishments. If you want to stand out, bring in new ideas for solving business problems.

BUSINESS EXECUTIVE WENDY BEECHAM'S APPROACH TO MEETING WITH YOUR BOSS

- What's the business issue, challenge, or opportunity?
- Why does it matter to the business?
- What needs to be done?
- What are your suggestions?

Don't backstab your boss, no matter how annoying and incompetent you may think they are, because it will get back to them. And don't surprise your boss. Keep them in the loop.

What bosses want are team members who are loyal and can help them accomplish their goals. They're looking for fresh ideas and people who create positive change. Diane, a senior vice president of HR at a software company, says bosses respect and take notice of employees who do everything well, including the grunt work.

Learn from your boss. Be open to his or her feedback. As

the old expression goes, "Feedback is a gift." Look for trends in the feedback you receive from your boss, mentors, colleagues, and others, then, work on those development areas.

If you can't get behind your boss, we have found you're better off looking for another opportunity. This will save you hours of unhappiness.

Keep in mind there are circumstances in which you *don't* need to make the relationship with your boss work, especially if your boss is a bully, unethical, or harassing you.

Suzanne, a young professional in the Bay Area, found herself in this situation. Her boss once told her in a meeting, "If you don't get me a drink, I'll grab your ass in front of all these people." She thought his inappropriate comments were only directed at her and found another job. Later, she ran into a woman in the department and learned that he had been saying inappropriate things to all of the women in the office. Her only regret is that she didn't stand up to him and tell him he was making her uncomfortable or report his behavior through the proper channels, such as HR.

If you are aligned with your boss, one of the benefits is he or she will prioritize time on their calendar for you. This is what Briana, a graduate of Emory University business school, found when doing a summer internship at Synopsys. "I believe my boss made time for me because I was professional, delivered my work assignments on time, and shared ideas that supported the team."

Occasionally in your career, you'll have a special boss who is just as invested in making the relationship work as you are.

For example, Luanne had a boss, Chuck, a senior vice

president at Cisco, who was very supportive of her success. When she went through the questions we've listed, he gave great advice: "Take risks, I'll support you. I'll never penalize you for making mistakes." She listened to him and consciously applied this mini-checklist. Over the course of four years, under his sponsorship, she was promoted four times, from senior manager to vice president.

Alice also had an exceptional boss, Rick, now a retired Cisco executive vice president, who has been a long-time mentor, coach, and sponsor. He is known as a leader committed to helping people become successful by providing regular coaching. She reported to him for seven years and, early on, he provided feedback that Alice could be overly sensitive at work. She adjusted and, over time, her work was rewarded with increased responsibility, excellent performance reviews, promotions, and a month-long job rotation in India.

5

Grow Your Professional Network

IN your career, individual performance will take you only so far. The savvy woman knows she needs other people, too, which is why building and growing your network is so important.

Networking is where the "guardian angels" of your career will be—and you never know when you're going to need one. You may find yourself in an unexpectedly tenuous work situation (think of the dot-com bubble burst in 2000 or the financial crisis of 2008) and be looking for a job. You may want to build your skills and increase your knowledge by reaching out to peers for best practices and advice. And you will certainly need mentors and coaches along the way. We all love our girlfriends, but you'll need more than your besties. Invest the time to build a professional network.

A lot of networking happens online, so have a killer LinkedIn profile. There's no excuse not to do this because it's so easy. You don't even have to leave your chair! Make sure your online profile is catchy, up to date, and reflects your career goals. Use SEO words so people with relevant opportunities, such as recruiters, can easily find you.

Of course, you will have to get out of your chair to network well. We've noticed that many men have a healthy attitude towards in-person networking. They look at it as a business transaction rather than an emotional investment. They're not looking for friends, necessarily. They're looking to connect with people who will provide a mutually beneficial business opportunity.

Learn to be comfortable networking at work-related events, whether it's business meetings, receptions, dinners, or other social events connected to work. A benchmark to think about is one networking event or activity a month. Most of us dread these events, but they are important for your career.

We realize it can be very intimidating to walk into a room of strangers or people you don't know well. We get nervous too! You might want to bring a colleague to make those early awkward moments easier—but force yourself to forge out on your own and meet new people. Luanne sets a goal of meeting three new people at each event and having a genuine conversation with each, then gives herself permission to leave. However, she often finds that once she gets the conversation going, she enjoys herself and stays longer than she thought she would.

Getting the conversation started is often the biggest challenge. In Debra Fine's book, *The Fine Art of Small Talk: How to Start a Conversation, Keep it Going, Build Networking Skills—and Leave a Positive Impression!*, she suggests the following questions to get the conversation going and avoid awkward silences:

* How did you become interested in_____?
* How did you get started in your business?
* Tell me what you enjoy most about your profession.

- Describe some of the challenges of your profession.

- How is your company different from the competition?

- What ways have you found to be the most effective in promoting your business?

- What advice would you give for someone just starting out in your business?

- What significant changes have you seen in your field in the past few years?

- What was the best job you ever had? What was your worst?

Once you've asked the question, listen! Adopting listening skills will make you a better communicator. Fine points out, "People want to be with people who make them feel special, not people who ARE special."

If you're an introvert, Susan Cain, author of *Quiet: The Power of Introverts in a World That Can't Stop Talking*, has two great tips. First, make a quota. Put a plan in place to attend one social event—one networking event, one party, something new—each week. A quota system sets you up so you don't feel guilty about not attending the events that exceed your quota. Second, reframe networking in a way that works for you. When you attend an event, create the "power of one" by looking for that kindred spirit you can connect with and have a real conversation. If you reach your quota of one person, you have accomplished what you needed to do. The pressure is off.

You can set time limits, too. When you decide ahead of time how long you'll stay at an event, it makes the commitment finite and much less intimidating, Jacqueline Whitmore, etiquette expert, author, and founder of The Protocol School of Palm Beach, blogs on Entrepreneur.com. "At a minimum, give yourself 20 minutes to get your nametag and grab a drink. Often, all you need is a few minutes to adjust to the environment." As Luanne pointed out, you may be surprised at how often you'll stay longer than planned.

You may not realize that you already have a rich network to tap into: your own. Make a list of all the people in your network: your parents, friends of your parents, your friends' parents, aunts and uncles, your alumni organization, past employers, athletic coaches, teachers, friends at the gym, your neighbors.

The people with whom you have strong ties are your personal network. Surprisingly, the power of networking doesn't usually come from your strong ties; it often comes from the people they are connected to, known as weak ties.

A famous 1973 study, "Getting a Job" by Mark Granovetter, a Stanford University professor and sociologist who immortalized the phrase "strength by weak ties," found that when it comes to finding out about jobs, new information, and new ideas, weak ties are generally more important than those you consider strong. This study found that 56% got jobs through a personal connection. Of those connections, most are weak ties.

Malcolm Gladwell, author of *The Tipping Point: How Little Things Can Make a Big Difference*, writes: "Think about it: many of your closest friends and contacts go to the same parties, do similar work, and exist in the same world as you. Weak ties, on the other hand, generally occupy a very different world than you. They're hanging out with different people with access to a whole inventory of knowledge and information unavailable to you and your close friends."

When you need something from someone in your network, all you need to do is ask. In our experience, people are receptive if you are sincere, direct, and specific about what you're asking for.

When asking, realize you also have a lot to offer. You are a valuable source of perspectives, current trends, and fresh ideas. In addition, people are always looking for talent; you may be the weak tie connection for someone else! So don't be shy in asking.

If you're feeling bold, you can be very assertive in building your network. For example, Tiffani Bova, Gartner vice president and distinguished analyst, started building her network of industry and professional contacts early in her career by boldly approaching keynote speakers at industry events to introduce herself and schedule mentoring sessions. Those contacts opened doors to more contacts and opportunities.

Tapping into your network is something that never ends, no matter where you are in your career.

When Luanne took on a new role as vice president of marketing for a networking security company in 2014, she reached out to a colleague and sales executive for advice on creating her 100-day marketing plan at a smaller company. She asked for his perspective on success strategies and building her plan. His advice was to keep the plan simple and execution-focused.

As Alice transitioned into consulting, her professional network has been her main source for consulting projects. She has also tapped into her network for advice on developing business proposals, establishing pricing strategies, managing business operations, and growing her consulting practice.

Remember that business etiquette applies to networking, too. As you meet people and as people help you, follow up with a quick "nice to meet you" or "thank you" email. Connect with them on LinkedIn. As you reach out to connect with people on LinkedIn, send a personal introductory note rather than using the generic template. Remind them of who you are and explain why you want to get connected.

If you're looking to build your network outside of the company where you work, there are many places to network with young professionals. Meet-up groups, Chambers of Commerce, college alumni organizations, and professional associations are a few possibilities to check into. There are also many business people to meet while volunteering at local food banks, homeless shelters, Habitat for Humanity, and similar philanthropic events. Volunteermatch.org is a great resource for finding activities and connecting with new people in your area.

If you want to differentiate yourself from your peers who are eating lunch at their desk every day, get out there and network. Net"work"ing is work. It's like going to the gym; it takes discipline to get the results you want. Schedule networking as part of your routine; you will be pleased at how it will pay off in your career.

THREE NEW PEOPLE I WANT TO MEET IN THE NEXT 3-6 MONTHS

_____

_____

_____

_____

_____

_____

6

Seek Out Mentors and Attract Sponsors

MENTORS and sponsors will accelerate your career—and you'll need both to get ahead. So what are mentors and sponsors, and what's the difference between the two?

	MENTOR	SPONSOR
ROLE:	A trusted adviser.	People in more senior positions who advocate for your career-growth opportunities and promotions.
PURPOSE:	Share their experience; provide guidance and advice.	Use their political influence to move you ahead.
ENGAGEMENT:	You seek mentors out; they can be situational or long-term.	They seek you out. There isn't an explicit conversation. They proactively take action to support you and your career.

In *The Glass Elevator: A Guide to Leadership Presence for Women on the Rise*, Ora Shtull suggests six areas to building your network of mentors and sponsors:

1. **Support:** who supports me personally at work?
2. **Expertise:** who shares knowledge or expertise with me?
3. **Influence:** who provides political support and influence on my behalf?
4. **Feedback:** who provides feedback and watches out for my career?
5. **Validation:** who makes me feel good about my work?
6. **Energy:** who helps me stay energized?

In her book, Shtull quotes research conducted by Rob Cross at the University of Virginia and Dr. Robert Thomas of the Accenture Institute of High Performance suggesting that your tribe will be infinitely stronger when you have two or three quality people fulfilling each of these six needs. That's somewhere between twelve to eighteen people to have an effective network.

How do you get a mentor? First, think about what you're looking for in a mentor. Is it career advice? Is it perspective on a particular situation? Once you know what you want, identify the person who can best mentor you. It could be someone inside or outside of your company.

Then ask them! If it's someone you know, reach out in person. Be specific about the advice you're seeking and how much of their time you're requesting. If you don't know them, reach out in person, by email, or with a personalized LinkedIn request. Tell them who you are, explain your connection, and ask them to be your mentor. When asking for their time, we'd suggest a 15-20-minute initial meeting. A successful mentoring relationship requires trust and chemistry. If you don't establish that in the beginning, you may want to find a mentor that's a better fit.

As you meet with your mentor, take the lead in scheduling time and arriving at meetings prepared with a list of questions. Also, find ways to support your mentor. It's not a one-way street.

"The best way to approach being useful to a mentor is to give help first," Keith Ferrazzi writes in *Never Eat Alone and Other Secrets to Success, One Relationship at a Time*. "If there is someone whose knowledge you need, find a way to be of use to that person. Consider their needs and how you can assist them. If you can't help them specifically, perhaps you can contribute to their charity, company or community. You have to be prepared to give back to your mentors and have them know that from the outset. If there are not immediate opportunities to help, you must be prudent and conscious of the imposition you're placing. If you are going to get someone's help, then at a minimum you should attempt to endear yourself to the mentor. Express gratitude, excitement and passion. Mentoring is a non-hierarchical activity that transcends careers and can cross organizational levels."

You can be of service to your mentor by being a sounding board for ideas or introducing them to someone in your network. Another idea is sharing ideas, articles, and books that may be interesting to your mentor. Shradha is a Santa Clara University graduate who approached Luanne for mentoring upon seeing her deliver a presentation. She introduced herself, and then followed up with an email asking for a 15-minute call to get Luanne's perspective on career and work-life balance. She also attached an article supporting what Luanne spoke about. She continued to follow up with relevant articles and books she thought Luanne would enjoy. In turn, Luanne helped her write her resume, served as a reference, and helped her negotiate her requirements for a new job.

By the way, don't be intimidated when asking someone to be your mentor. Many people who are more established get great satisfaction from mentoring and helping others in their careers—including us!

Alice had listed "mentoring and coaching" as one of her skills on Cisco's internal company directory and received a call from Surja, a systems engineer in Chicago who wanted to become a better communicator. They had monthly phone calls in which they discussed Surja's personal brand and communications style. Over the course of a year, Surja updated her professional photo and wardrobe and became more strategic when speaking up at meetings and presenting. Surja's commitment and genuine appreciation for the coaching made the investment of time more than worthwhile for Alice.

Mentors can often see behaviors that may be holding you back. Maxine, an Australian entrepreneur, confided with us that she wishes she had understood the importance of a mentor in her first job out of college. In her first two years, she advanced quickly and was promoted from programmer to project manager to data analyst. Then, she hit a wall. Her boss thought she was doing such a great job that she didn't want to let go of her; she blocked opportunities. Two years later, Maxine took a job in another organization as a lateral move. A mentor could have helped her navigate an open conversation with her boss and move through that roadblock.

With sponsorship, your role is to demonstrate leadership qualities, be visible, and consistently deliver results. "Sponsors are powerful leaders who see potential in you and, provided you give them 110 percent, will go out on a limb to make things happen for you," writes Sylvia Ann Hewlett, an author on executive presence.

You don't ask someone to be your sponsor the way you'd ask someone to be your mentor. They find you. This is why consistently delivering great results and commanding executive presence are so crucial. Powerful people will take notice. You will typically be aware when someone influential begins playing a sponsorship role for you, even though it's not explicit or articulated. They won't approach you and ask to be your sponsor. Behind the scenes, a sponsor is bringing your name up and actively advocating for you for promotions, new roles, and interesting assignments. As you get the sense that a senior person is providing sponsorship for you, stay visible and invest in that relationship so they continue to be aware of the impact you're having. Sponsorship can be a fast track to the top.

7

Negotiate Everything: "Asking" is a business skill

NEGOTIATIONS are often awkward for women. Many women don't want to be perceived as demanding or ungrateful by "asking" for anything more than what is offered. "It can make you feel bad," says Kim, A U.C. Santa Cruz graduate in Silicon Valley. "It's not a skill you learn in college," says Katie in Chicago. Yes, it can be uncomfortable and unfamiliar, but avoiding negotiations in the hopes of avoiding conflict or embarrassment is a big mistake.

Why is negotiation so important?

First, the ability to negotiate is a critical business skill. You need to show you're capable of it.

Second, many men are champs at it, and they may be out-negotiating you for similar jobs. Men are typically raised to negotiate well and without emotion. Women fall behind men every step of the way because they simply don't ask.

In the book, *Women Don't Ask: Negotiation and the Gender Divide*, Linda Babcock and Sara Laschever report an average 7.4% difference between the starting salaries for male and female MBAs. Men initiate negotiations four times as often as women. Those who negotiated were able to increase their salary by more than seven percent.

That 7.4% makes a huge difference over time. Dr. Margaret Neale, a professor at the Stanford Graduate School of Business, writes on Forbes.com, "One of the things I ask my students is: If you think of a $100,000 salary, and one person negotiates and gets $107,000, and the other doesn't—what's the cost of that? If you and your counterpart who negotiated are treated identically by the company—you are given the same raises and promotions—35 years later, you will have to work eight more years to be as wealthy as your counterpart at retirement."

Ok. Have we convinced you? You need to separate your personal feelings about "asking" and make this a business transaction. "In negotiations, you need to separate 'what I want' from 'how I feel,'" says Monica, a Bay Area professional. "Speak in the language of business, not feelings."

The most successful negotiations are a "win-win" for both parties. Throughout the entire negotiation, both parties emphasize the benefit to each other. Jessica, CEO of a high tech firm, said: "Do you know how many people ask me for things every day? I have to consider, 'What's in it for my company and me?'" If you're asking for a promotion, for example, let your boss know how much more you'll deliver for the business with more responsibility.

If you're not comfortable negotiating, start experimenting.

At the farmer's market, ask if you can get three apples for the price of two. Call your mobile service provider and, if you've been a loyal customer, ask for a better pricing package. At a department store, ask if there are any discounts available you can apply to your purchase.

Let's apply negotiating to the business world. Your first negotiation will most likely be your salary. Here's how to prepare for that conversation:

- Research salary. Check sites like glassdoor.com, payscale.com, and theladders.com. Know that salary ranges are dependent on cost of living for different parts of the country (for example, salaries will be higher in Silicon Valley than in a small town in Maine).

- Do the math and decide what your deal breaker point is. What's the lowest salary you'll accept?

- Be aware that most companies have a salary range for each position. There is room to negotiate based on the candidate's level of education, experience, certifications, potential, and, sometimes, how quickly the company needs to fill the role.

- Money is not the only negotiable currency . . . sign-on bonus, cell phone, paid time off, tuition reimbursement, and working from home are also negotiable.

- Focus negotiations on the value you provide, not your personal expenses (for example, high rent, student loans, car payment, the cost of the city you'll be working in).

- Project a confident tone. You don't want to sound tentative, hesitant, or overly grateful; you also don't want to sound entitled. Be clear and direct. Don't ramble. Get yourself into a frame of mind that's as matter-of-fact as if you were asking if there's free parking validation for your movie tickets.

- Practice out loud before you have the actual conversation. The way you present yourself and the words you use matter.

- Negotiate in person or by phone; not over email.

- Once you receive a verbal offer, ask for it in writing. You can circle back for clarification and even further negotiation if the entire compensation package is different than what you understood in the conversation.

QUESTIONS	YOUR RESPONSE
What are your salary expectations?	"I've researched the average salary for this role. Given my experience, I'm confident I'd fall at the higher end of the range. My salary expectation is $$$."(Give a number—ask high so there is room to negotiate.)
We'd like to offer you a job. The salary is $$$.	"I'm really excited about this offer. My understanding is the initial offer is usually in the middle of your salary range. I'm highly motivated and have a lot to offer. Is there room to negotiate?" If they say no, ask, "What's a reasonable expectation for salary increases?" Or, "I understand. Is there flexibility for me to work from home one day a week (or another negotiable item)?"

When negotiating, the worst that can happen is they say no. But you've demonstrated you are confident enough to negotiate—and those in power will respect you more for asking.

8

Dress for Success

THIS is probably our most controversial topic because it's so personal and women have so many choices when it comes to how they dress. The bottom line is we are all noticed and judged for our appearance, and research shows it has a lot do with success. The goal is to have impact with your ideas and professional skills, not your outfit. The visual message you want to send is that you're savvy and perceptive: you understand the importance of showing up at work professionally dressed.

How you dress is an expression of your personality and your brand. We're all for being fashionable and unique. You can play up femininity, if you choose, by wearing skirts and dresses and fun jewelry. Have your own sense of style. Go for a signature look. What woman doesn't appreciate a genuine compliment on her appearance? A new outfit can be a total pick-me-up. Luanne and Alice have been known for a doing little "retail therapy" at the end of a tough day. Kidding aside, we both consider our attire a strategic part of our professional brands so we've invested time, money, and attention to it.

When it comes to appropriate dress at work, there are no absolutes. There are clearly differences between what's appropriate in Silicon Valley and on Wall Street. There are cultural differences, too. But here are two landmines to absolutely avoid.

First, don't play up your sexuality in the office. Work isn't Hollywood. Men—and women!—are easily distracted by the woman who is too sexy in the office. Even kids notice! Here's a great quote from Monica, a Bay Area schoolteacher: "Kids are the first to say, 'Your bra is showing!'"

Second, don't be too casual. Wearing workout clothes and yoga pants to work is at odds with taking work seriously. Samantha, a specialist for a small real estate marketing firm, says covering visible tattoos in certain work environments and situations is also a good idea. You never know when you might be called into a meeting with senior management or a customer.

Considering that half the workforce is men (and they represent 85% of executive positions, according to Catalyst), we thought it was critical to get their candid view.

When we asked men what they thought when they saw a woman who is inappropriately dressed at work, here are some of their answers:

- "It shows she cares more about what she's wearing than her work."
- "She's immature; an amateur. She's not versed in how to show up at work. It makes me question her capabilities and makes me wonder how much responsibility I should give to her."
- "She lacks a strong mentor in her life."
- "She must be playing to her only strength."

- "I think the same thing I think when I see a man who is inappropriately dressed; they don't take their job seriously. I also find these people commonly do not communicate effectively or work well with others. Their lack of understanding of how their dress impacts people's impressions of them tends not to be their only blind spot when it comes to human interaction."

- "Strive to be known for your IQ, not your cup size, as it's hard enough to build a reputation, but it is twice as hard to rebuild one," was the colorful advice of one male colleague.

When we asked if they'd share those opinions with women, they said it's "dangerous waters." One man said, "The legal liability is too high and the rules too subjective for me to comment." Another said, "There is no upside for me but huge risk."

Every morning that you go into the office, take the time to think about what you're wearing and the messages you're sending about yourself as a professional. "Think of your wardrobe as marketing," says brand expert William Arruda. "Your clothes and your accessories do the same thing for your personal brand." You may also want to ask a mentor or a trusted colleague what messages you are sending with your attire. Then ask yourself, do those messages line up with your personal brand?

DO	DON'T
Have your own sense of style that's consistent with your brand; have a polished, professional look.	Wear clothes that are too tight, too sexy, too sheer, too short, show too much cleavage.
Make a feminine statement with makeup, a fun necklace, jewelry, color.	Dress for a night out with five-inch platforms, excessive makeup, flashy jewelry, and strong fragrance.
Know the difference between business attire (suits with a skirt or pants, nice dresses, dressy separates, heels) and business casual (khakis, nice jeans without holes).	Be too casual (beachwear, shorts, casual t-shirts, sweat shirts, flip flops, yoga pants, and work-out clothes are not appropriate at work).
Dress up for a job interview. Your overall look should be simple and polished. Err on the more conservative side, even if you're interviewing at a Google or Facebook. For example, a dress or skirt is dressier than pants; a jacket is dressier than a cardigan sweater. Putting effort into dressing up is a sign of respect to the person you're interviewing with. It shows you want the job and you're taking the interview seriously.	This isn't the time for short hemlines, accessories that are too casual or too distracting (e.g., dangly jewelry, clanking bracelets).
Dress for the job you want, not the job you have.	Dress as if you are headed to the gym or just rolled out of bed.

9

Practice Good Business Etiquette

JUST like your appearance, you are also judged for demonstrating business etiquette. If you don't have a firm handshake, don't know which bread plate is yours at a business dinner, and never send thank you notes, it's a poor reflection on your professional brand. And, similar to attire, it's doubtful anyone will call you on it.

Demonstrating proper business protocol shows you can operate successfully in today's multi-cultural, multi-generational work environment.

Peter and Peggy Post, the great grandchildren of Emily Post, the famous etiquette expert, have written a great reference book, *The Etiquette Advantage in Business: Personal Skills for Professional Success.* "Etiquette is not about rules," they write. "Etiquette is about building relationships, plain and simple. Etiquette gives us clues as to how we should act and what we should do in any given situation, so that we can be as successful as possible in our interactions with the people around us. Far from stifling your personality in a straitjacket of do's and don'ts, etiquette—by giving you the confidence to handle a wide variety of situations with ease and aplomb—actually lets you focus on being your relaxed self."

The Posts organize business etiquette into actions, appearance, and words. They explain, "One of the hallmarks of good etiquette is it never calls attention to itself. When everything is going well as far as your actions, appearance, and words are concerned, your focus—and the focus of the people you are with—will be on the content of your discussion. Slip up with any of these factors, however, and the focus will suddenly shift to the failure ('I can't believe she just did that.')."

If you want the straight scoop, the Posts' book provides guidance on numerous situations, from deciding what to wear to hosting, attending, and speaking at the perfect meeting. There's also a helpful chapter on doing business in another country and working with people from different cultures.

Here are the most common business situations you'll encounter as you begin your career.

SITUATION	ETIQUETTE
JOB INTERVIEW	Show up 10 minutes early. Wear business attire (even if the work atmosphere is casual). Bring a hard copy of your resume and professional business cards if you have them. Promptly write a customized email thank you note to each person you met with. Extra credit for handwritten thank you notes.

SITUATION	ETIQUETTE
BUSINESS DINNER	Know how a table is set:

Food is placed to the left of the dinner plate. The words "food" and "left" each have four letters; if the table is set properly, your bread or salad or any other food dish will be placed to the left of your dinner plate. Similarly, drinks are placed to the right of the dinner plate, and the words "glass" and "right" contain five letters. Any glass or drink will be placed to the right of the dinner plate.

Left and right also work for your utensils. Your fork (four letters) goes to the left; your knife and spoon (five letters each) go to the right.

Also, think "BMW" when trying to remember where to place plates and glasses. Bread-and-butter plate is on the left, meal is in the middle, water glass is on the right.

SITUATION	ETIQUETTE
ALCOHOL	Enjoy a glass of wine or two, but never get drunk at a work event. There's still a double standard: men can get away with it; women can't. Here's a perfect story for you. We attended a work event where a male executive and female mid-level manager were drinking and dirty dancing on a table in a bar in front of dozens of co-workers. Much to the enjoyment of the audience, the table broke. The next day, it was a big topic of conversation. He was patted on the back for his antics, yet people were embarrassed for her. The moral of this story isn't 'don't dance on tables,' it's don't get drunk at work functions. Period.
GOSSIP	Your words are part of your brand. If you gossip, it's a reflection on you. When in doubt, refrain from venting about your co-workers. You never know when your IM is appearing on a WebEx screen, your email is forwarded, or your words from last week's happy hour are repeated.
HUG OR HAND SHAKE?	In general, girls have not been taught to shake hands, and so at work we're often uncomfortable when deciding whether to hug or shake hands. Always shake and do it confidently! A proper handshake requires looking someone in the eyes and firmly shaking their hand. No wimpy shakes. Practice on someone if you are not comfortable.

SITUATION	ETIQUETTE
HUGGING	We are huggers! Please see Tim Sackett's list—so funny and so true!
THANK YOU'S	For important correspondence, email is better than text. Make your thank you notes short, sincere, and personal. Be prompt, within 24 hours of the interaction. Be sure to use spelling/grammar check.
GIFT GIVING AT THE OFFICE	It is not required or expected. If there is a team gift, feel free to contribute. Personal gifts to colleagues are not considered a company business expense.
INTERNATIONAL ETIQUETTE	If you're traveling internationally for work, here's a helpful website for business protocol and customs around the world: www.culturecrossing.net

11 RULES FOR HUGGING AT WORK
TIM SACKETT, PRESIDENT,
HRU TECHNICAL RESOURCES

1. Don't hug those you supervise. (The caveats: You can hug a subordinate if it's being supportive in a non-creepy way (major family or personal loss—sideways, kind of arm around the shoulder, you care about them hug); it's at a wedding and you are congratulating them; it's a hug for a professional win (promotion, giant sale, big project completion, etc.) and it's with a group, not alone in your office with the lights off; you would feel comfortable with your spouse standing next you and watching that specific hug.)

2. Hug your external customers or clients when they initiate a hugging sequence. (The caveats: Don't hug if: it is required to get business—that's not hugging, that's harassment. Don't let the hug last more than a second or two, or it gets creepy. Don't mention the hug afterwards; that makes you seem creepy!)

3. Don't hug the person you're having an affair with in the office. (No explanation needed.)

4. Hug peers, just not every day. (It's all right to hug, but you don't need to do it every day for people you see daily. Save some up and make it special!)

5. When you hug, hug for real. (Nothing worse than the 'fake hug'! A fake hug is worse than a non-hug.)

6. Don't whisper, 'You smell good,' when hugging someone professionally. (That's creepy—in fact don't whisper anything while hugging!)

7. Don't close your eyes while hugging professionally. (That's weird and a bit stalker-ish.)

8. It is all right to announce a hug is coming. (Some people will appreciate a 'Hey, Come here. I'm giving you a hug—it's been a long time!')

9. It's never all right to hug from behind. (Creepier!)

10. Never hug in the restroom. (It makes for awkward moments when other employees walk in and see that.)

11. If you're questioning yourself whether it will be all right to hug someone professionally, that is your cue that it probably isn't.

The polished, professional woman knows that good manners can set her apart. At work, consideration of others means being on time, paying attention in meetings, and avoiding texting during conversations. Remember, "good manners and kindness are always in fashion."

10

Be a Rock Star Communicator

THE number one skill that employers look for in hiring mid-level managers is oral communication skills across nearly all industries, according to the 2014 Corporate Recruiters Survey Report. On average, employers ranked communication skills twice as important as managerial skills in this report.

So if you want to be employable, influential, and powerful, practice your communication skills! We're not just talking about formal presentations either. "Every time you open your mouth in public, you are a public speaker," writes Timothy Koegel in *The Exceptional Presenter.*

Author Sylvia Ann Hewlett agrees: "Most of us tend to think of communication skills in terms of formal presentation skills. But when are you not on stage? When are you not being judged? No matter what your job title or how junior or senior you are, you are always presenting. Whether it's a quick email to your boss, a casual comment you make to your colleagues in the hallway, or a pitch you prepare for clients, you're conveying who you are and what authority is your due. In the real world and very much in the virtual one, every verbal encounter is a vital opportunity to create and nurture a positive impression."

In everyday conversations and office communications:

- Speak plain English. Don't get sucked into the vortex of corporate speak and jargon! You know the words: streamline, maximize, optimize. Or the "inside baseball" phrases that are only used within a particular group or organization. You will lose your audience. Use the same day-to-day conversational language you would use with a friend; it's easier for your audience to understand.

- Use your voice for greater impact. Variety is key. Mix up your voice pitch, your tone, and your volume. Add pauses for emphasis.

- Use powerful words (e.g., lead, build, create, decide) versus weak words (e.g., help, support).

- Avoid self-defeating language. Don't qualify what you're saying with "I think..." or "This probably isn't a very good idea, but..." and don't ask for permission to ask a question. Simply state, "I have a question..."

- Delete fillers (e.g., um, ah, like, you know) and words that add no meaning (e.g., really, actually, clearly, "right?").

- Don't let your voice inflection go up at the end of a sentence. This is a common issue for women. It does not sound confident.

When presenting, whether you're speaking up in a team meeting or delivering a speech in front of an audience, the fundamentals are the same.

First, understand your audience. "I have seen a lot of good, smart people stall their careers because they talk too much or they don't get to the point," says Mary Brienza CEO, NYSE Regulation, Inc. in the book *The Glass Elevator: A Guide to Leadership Presence for Women on the Rise.* "They don't read their audience and, therefore, can't convey what their audience needs to hear! You have to tailor, slice, dice, and deliver your message to succeed."

If you're not familiar with your audience, do some research and talk to people to understand what's on their minds. Your audience will be more receptive if they feel your message is tailored for them.

Next, spend time planning what you will say. We've all seen speakers who ramble with no point. Here's a simple process for delivering a compelling talk:

- Clarify your objective. What do you want your audience to think, feel, or believe at the end of your talk?

- Have a clear point of view. Don't simply share data and statistics. Have an opinion or perspective and support it with evidence.

- Prepare an outline. Create a storyline; write it down. You can use the format we all learned in school: an introduction (where you will share your point of view), three parts for the body, and a conclusion.

- Be creative and memorable. Use anecdotes, personal stories, relevant quotes, humor, or pose a rhetorical question to engage your audience. The purpose here isn't simply to be creative; make a clear connection to business impact.

Spend time practicing your delivery. How you deliver a message can have more impact than the message itself. Here are few lessons we've learned from our years presenting:

- Dress like a pro. According to Malcolm Gladwell, in *Blink: The Power of Thinking Without Thinking*, first impressions occur instantaneously; they are unconscious and happen "without thinking." Think about the impression you will make as you walk on stage. Wear flattering clothes and a bra with thicker material to hide any awkward moments. We attended a presentation where a female executive didn't heed this advice, which led to a very distracted and uncomfortable audience watching her on the i-mag screen. It's fine to wear a statement piece, but don't overdue the bling and wear noisy bangles. Also, avoid fabrics such as silk that show perspiration.

- Stand tall. Having good posture not only sends a message of confidence, it also makes it easier to breathe—which is important for relaxing while speaking.

- Get comfortable with your presentation stance. This is how you stand when you're not gesturing. It looks most natural to have your hands at your sides in a relaxed pose. This doesn't feel natural at first, so practice this pose before you get up in front of an audience.

- Speak slowly and clearly; enunciate your words. When we're nervous, we tend to rush. Confident people take their time. Slow down, breathe deeply, and take your time.

- Maintain good eye contact with your audience. This is one of the most important elements for engaging your audience. Don't spend the entire time looking at your boss or your best friend in the front row. Look to people across the entire room and hold each gaze for a few seconds before you look to the next person.

- Use the floor space. Don't stand in one place. On the other hand, don't pace back and forth. Find a comfortable place and speak for a while. Then, as you're transitioning to your next thought or section, move to another part of the room or stage.

- Avoid notes or index cards in your hands. If your hands are trembling due to an adrenaline rush, your nervousness will be apparent in your shaking cards. If you are well prepared, you won't need a crutch.

We can't emphasize enough the importance of practicing. Prepare notes and rehearse by yourself or, ideally, in front of others. Videotape yourself, if possible. You want to get to a point where you've internalized your main messages and can speak about them naturally without sounding memorized or scripted. It's about being prepared. It's risky to wing it.

If you're nervous about public speaking (which is totally normal), take a few deep breaths, shake your limbs to get rid of nervous energy, and eat a mint to avoid dry mouth.

Matt Abrahams, author of *Speaking Up Without Freaking Out: 35 Techniques for Confident, Calm, and Competent Presenting*, offers these suggestions for managing nerves:

- The "P, B & J Approach": Practice, Breathe, and Just Do It!

- During your presentation, give your nervous energy a place to go by squeezing your toes or thumb and pointer finger with your non-gesturing hand.

- Chunk your presentation into key ideas so it's easier to remember.

- Rehearse and "over learn" so your delivery becomes

automated, which frees you to be more natural and to ad lib a bit when presenting. However, avoid memorizing. Memorizing invites performance anxiety where there is a right way (the way memorized) versus a wrong way to say something. Memorization forces people to be remote from their audience because they are speaking to them through a script. The best approach is to be very familiar with your topic and to speak to an overall storyline with key messages.

- Before you speak, avoid carbohydrates (which make you sluggish) and caffeine (which makes you wired); eat complex carbohydrates (which stabilize your blood sugar and give you energy); take a probiotic (which reduces stress-inducing hormones).

As a communications and public speaking coach, Alice has been working with Silicon Valley executives for more than 20 years. Some spend months preparing their content and rehearsing for major presentations so their delivery will look effortless. One executive practiced his speeches while running on the treadmill.

When Alice prepares for her own presentations, she creates a word document of key messages for each slide. As she gets more comfortable practicing the key messages, she narrows her "cheat sheet" down to key words. Once she has the structure of key words in her mind, she can improvise when delivering the speech before an audience. So much of successful public speaking is practice and preparation.

Luanne has delivered presentations all over the world. She prepares by printing out the slides and the notes and practicing while blasting music and working out on the elliptical. It works for her! She also makes sure she has a strong opening story to help her to relax as she starts her presentation and takes a few deep breaths before she steps on stage to get the excess adrenaline out of her system. By the way, the first few minutes are the hardest of the presentation for everyone.

Public speaking is a key area to develop for career success. Push yourself to work on it. Develop expertise by becoming an active observer. Watch people at work or view TED Talks. Here are a few of our favorites for both content and delivery: "Your Body Language Shapes Who You Are," by Amy Cuddy. "Why We Have Too Few Women Leaders," by Sheryl Sandberg. "The Power of Vulnerability," by Brené Brown. "The Danger of a Single Story," by Chimamanda Ngozi Adichie. Notice what speakers do and don't do well, and learn from it.

Before we wrap up, a word on the written word. Alice is convinced strong writing skills are essential for success in the business world, even if you're not in communications. Solid writing demonstrates your ability to think strategically, be influential, and convey your ideas. Typos, grammar errors, and run-on sentences send signals that your work is sloppy and you may not be organized in your thinking. Review your work emails to assess if your writing is clear, succinct, and error-free.

We want to leave you with three thoughts. First, this is one of our largest chapters because we believe it is one of the most important skills to master for a successful career. Second, we're not alone; as you remember, it's the number one skill employers look for when hiring. Third, who are the inspirational leaders you admire? Our guess is they are great communicators. The good news is that anyone can become a more accomplished communicator. It takes practice! So stick with it.

The Exceptional Presenter Is:

- **Organized.** Exceptional Presenters Take Charge! They look poised and polished. They sound prepared. You get the sense they are not there to waste time. Their goal is not to overwhelm, but to inform, persuade, influence, entertain or enlighten. Their message is well structured and clearly defined.

- **Passionate.** Exceptional presenters exude enthusiasm and conviction. If the presenter doesn't look and sound passionate about his or her topic, why would anyone else be passionate about it? Exceptional presenters speak from the heart and leave no doubt as to where they stand. Their energy is persuasive and contagious.

- **Engaging.** Exceptional presenters do everything in their power to engage each audience member. They build rapport quickly and involve the audience early and often. If you want their respect, you must first connect.

- **Natural.** An exceptional presenter's style is natural. Their delivery has a conversational feel. Natural presenters make it look easy. They appear comfortable with any audience. A presenter who appears natural appears confident.

As an exceptional presenter, you must:

- **Understand Your Audience.** Exceptional presenters learn as much as they can about their audiences before they present to them. The more they know about the audience, the easier it will be to connect and engage.

- **Practice.** Those who practice improve. Those who don't, don't. Exceptional skills must become second nature. The time to practice is during your normal daily routines, when habits can be formed and mistakes are not costly.

—excerpt from *The Exceptional Presenter* by Timothy Koegel

11

Stand Out; Be Visible

AS women, many of us have been raised to believe that if we work hard enough, we'll get the recognition we deserve. Unfortunately, that's not the case at work. "I used to think that if you put in your time, good things will come to you," said Aly, a Cal Poly graduate and healthcare recruiter. "I realize in the work world you've got to share your ideas and be passionate about your role. Recognition comes to those who stand out."

A big part of visibility is speaking up, and this is an area many women struggle with. A 2014 Harvard Business Review study based on 7,000 surveys and interviews with 1,100 female executives found that "women often have a hard time making their otherwise strong voices heard in meetings, either because they're not speaking loudly enough or because they can't find a way to break into the conversation at all." When male peers were interviewed, "more than a third indicated that when their female peers do speak up, they fail to articulate a strong point of view. Half said that women allow themselves to be interrupted, apologize repeatedly, and fail to back up opinions with evidence." Several men reported seeing "a female colleague get rattled and remain silent even when she was the expert at the table."

Early in your career is the perfect time to get comfortable speaking up. Share your ideas, opinions, and what you know in meetings. Ask your manager for candid feedback on how you can improve your participation impact and speaking skills. Raise your hand. Be the one who shows initiative, joins the special project, and takes on assignments outside of your day-to-day role. Be creative in initiating solutions and solving problems.

Keep in mind that you don't need permission to create change that has a positive business impact. Susan, a vice president at a fast-growing IT software and services company, said that once a younger woman on her team asked for her executive support in trying out a new idea. She told her, "Just do it. You don't need my ok. You're already empowered!"

Another great opportunity for getting noticed is leading a virtual team. When Alice was managing communications for Cisco's top sales executive, she built a virtual team of the 20 communications managers supporting sales leaders across the globe. She created a compelling purpose by sharing information and creating a sense of community that brought the team together, even though they didn't report to her. Alice went beyond the scope of her job description and stepped into a leadership role on her own. Ultimately, it led to a broader role where she led a global team of the directors leading communications for each of the company's business functions.

Standing out sometimes requires being your own PR agent.

"How do you promote your successes and wins in the office environment without it sounding like bragging?" asked Emily, who is a student at the Academy of Art University in San Francisco.

Make sure your boss is aware of your results and the impact you're having, and that your work is helping your boss and the company achieve their business objectives. Share your successes in your one-on-one meetings with your boss, or drop him or her a short email. Keep track of your accomplishments throughout the year so you've got them in one place when it's time for your year-end appraisal. Be confident in sharing your successes at team meetings.

Also, have others sing your praises. If you are a dedicated team player who is doing excellent work, chances are others are commenting about how great you are. It's the best PR you can get!

12

Recover Well from Disappointments and Mistakes

YOU need to take risks if you want to get ahead. And if you're taking risks, you're going to make mistakes. Mistakes are proof that you're taking action. They can be positive if you learn from them.

Many women make the mistake, so to speak, of taking their mistakes personally. Some women agonize over their mistakes for days, months, even years, which is a huge confidence buster and waste of precious time. "It's especially difficult if it's a public mistake," says Rachel, who just graduated from University of Michigan. "You feel it's your fault. Your perception of the situation impacts your future steps. It has a ripple effect and can undermine your confidence from taking future risks."

No one is exempt. We've witnessed senior executives literally fall on their faces as they were getting on stage to make a presentation. A colleague of ours meant to send a confidential email to an executive and accidentally sent it to his entire organization. A woman we know accepted an offer for a new role in her company. As she was accepting the offer, she mentioned she was expecting an external offer, thinking it would make her more desirable. Her internal offer was immediately rescinded and she was out of a job. Then there are the everyday mishaps, like mispronouncing names and words, embarrassing typos on presentations and emails, humor that falls flat. We all face disappointments in our career, too: the job you don't get, the mediocre job review, the startup that goes bust.

As Darren Hardy, publisher of *SUCCESS Magazine*, points out: "Failure is an event, not a person."

Think of Michael Jordan, considered one of the best basketball players of all time. He won six NBA championships and five regular season MVP awards. He said, "I've missed more than 9,000 shots in my career. I've lost almost 300 games. Twenty-six times, I've been trusted to take the game winning shot . . . and missed. I've failed over and over and over again in my life. And that is why I succeed."

Luanne had an experience of making a big presentation in front of a large audience with senior business leaders sitting in the front row. She saw them making critical comments to each other about her content, which flustered her. And it showed. One of the sales leaders came up to her after the presentation and said, "Well, that didn't go so well. But brush it off. You know what you're doing." Luanne was bummed out for a day, then resolved to not be intimidated or to reveal her emotions the next time she was criticized in public.

"Anyone who accomplishes great things in business and in life is bound to fail along the way," says Marie Forleo, described by Oprah as a thought leader for the next generation. "Feeling like a failure is a natural part of success. It's actually a good thing. It means you're taking action and putting yourself out there, which is more than most critics and naysayers have the balls to do. Feeling like a failure is normal. It means you're human like the rest of us. Feeling like a failure often means you're moments from your biggest success."

The healthy way to manage setbacks is to accept them and handle them with grace. For example, one of the executives who fell on stage made light of it, even though it was pretty humiliating. The other executive recovered quickly, then moved right into her presentation as if it was no big deal. She didn't turn it into her most embarrassing moment. How you handle your mistakes and disappointments is what will set you apart as thoughtful, professional, and mature.

Here are the main points to keep in mind for managing setbacks:

- Acknowledge your mistake. Take responsibility without beating yourself up. Don't blame others. On the other hand, there's no need to over-apologize (another female tendency).

- Give yourself a set amount of time to agonize. Set aside 24 hours to be miserable—then, let it go. There's no benefit to hitting the replay button again and again.

- Learn from it. Write down what you learned and what you would do differently next time. Ask your boss and mentors for feedback and perspective.

Most of us spend 90% of the time reliving the accident and only 10% on what we learned. Don't be so hard on yourself! Everybody makes mistakes. Look forward, not backward. Just because you failed yesterday doesn't mean you won't be successful tomorrow.

13

Be Politically Smart

OFFICE politics are everywhere. You can't escape them.

"Trying to avoid office politics is like trying to avoid the weather," says Dr. Lois Frankel in her book *Nice Girls Don't Get the Corner Office: 101 Unconscious Mistakes Women Make that Sabotage Their Careers.*

What are office politics? "It's how things get done in the workplace, in government, in professional organizations," Frankel explains. "If you're not involved in office politics, you're not playing the game. The business of politics is simply the business of relationships, an understanding of the quid pro quo, something in exchange for something else (inherent to every relationship)."

As you start your career, you may wonder what you have to offer in this "quid pro quo" (or "this for that") exchange? You bring plenty to the table. Do your job well; your manager provides a good review or salary increase in exchange. Raise your hand to do a project outside of your current role; you get exposure with a new chain of command. Be a good team player; you create a community of support amongst your peers.

Amy Schulman, a venture partner at Polaris Partners,

shared a great metaphor for explaining the "quid pro quo" concept in a 2013 *The New York Times* article: "One thing that happens at work is that women tend to hoard favors as if they were airline miles—you know, the hundreds of thousands of airplane miles that we're saving for when we really need them. But 'when we really need them' may never come. The trips are not going to happen, and we'll be left with 800,000 airline miles. There's a parallel at work. You need to spend political capital—be unafraid to introduce people, compliment somebody when it's deserved and stand up for something you really believe in, rather than just go with the flow. I don't mean being a perennial troublemaker, but it's about having conviction and courage. Spend that political capital you earn by being intellectually credible, by being a fighter for the people on your team when appropriate, and by arguing for principles that matter. Those are qualities that give you credit."

This all sounds perfectly fair on paper. So why all the negative emotions associated with office politics such as anxiety, frustration, and feeling blindsided? The reason is because people are angling for power all the time—often, at your expense. You have to rise above it and demonstrate you're savvy enough to see the politics at play and navigate them with confidence.

The toughest book we've seen on this topic is *The 48 Laws of Power* by Robert Greene. "No one wants less power; everyone wants more," he writes. "Power is a game—this cannot be repeated too often—and in games you do not judge your opponents by their intentions but by the effect of their actions. You measure their strategy and their power by what you can see and feel. Everything must appear civilized, decent, democratic, and fair. But if we play by those rules too strictly, if we take them too literally, we are crushed by those around us who are not so foolish."

In mastering the game of power, many of his 48 laws are straight out of an episode of Netflix's *House of Cards*. His book is a bit dark because it's ruthless but we found it well worth the read because it's a wake-up call about how power works.

There are as many political plots and players as there are people in the workforce. Each situation is unique. Here are the most common we've seen and ideas on how to come out ahead:

- Changing winds. The work landscape is changing and the person who has hired you has left, you have a new boss, there's been a reorg, or your company that's been on a growth path is suddenly not doing so well. Be aware of what's happening around you by staying connected to people in power and those around them. Also, don't align with just one powerful person. Power dynamics can change quickly, and a person in power can fall out of favor. Avoid being blindsided by big changes by staying connected.

- Working with people you don't like. It would be so nice to walk away from the people who drive us crazy! Unfortunately, in the real world, you've got to figure out how to make key relationships work, says Jeffrey Pfeffer in his book *Power: Why Some People Have It And Others Don't*. He quotes Gary Loveman, CEO and President of Caesars Entertainment Corporation: "There comes a point in your career where you simply have to make critical relationships work. Your feelings, or for that matter, others' feelings about you, don't matter. To be successful, you have to get over resentments, jealousies, anger, or anything else that might get in the way of building a relationship where you can get the resources necessary to get the job done." In addition, don't be contemptuous to those who disagree with you. It's easy to assume those with a different perspective are somehow not as smart, informed, or as perceptive as we are.

- Dealing with the bitch. It's a shame we have to call this out, but we've seen it too many times to ignore. To be successful, you have to be aggressive and stand up for yourself in the business world. But that's not what we're talking about here. The telltale sign of a bitch is a woman who is competitive with other women. She is ambitious and threatened by your power. She will question your authority and competency; you will have to watch your back. She may or may not report to you and may or may not be in your department. You're often left wondering, *What did I do to create this?* You probably didn't do anything at all, and take comfort in the fact that other people recognize this woman and how she operates over time. Don't stoop to the level of gossip and schoolyard fights. Your protection is doing great work and being a role model for positive energy. Luanne had one of these women join her team following a reorganization. She—we'll call her *B*—made it clear she didn't want to be part of Luanne's team. In their initial meeting, *B* said she preferred to work for men. She made venomous digs and was divisive. The team felt they constantly had to be on alert. Ultimately, *B* left the company. Looking back, Luanne wishes she had spent less time and energy on trying to make the situation work and more time setting boundaries on how this woman was treating her colleagues.

- Losing your power. "Power is lost because changed circumstances render previous skills or networks obsolete or because people may acquire positions without learning enough about power dynamics in their organization," Jeffrey Pfeffer writes in his book on power. Invest in developing a strong professional network, both inside and outside your company, and continually developing your professional skills.

A few of our strategies for navigating power in the workplace are:

- Be aware of who has the power and get close to them and those around them. Power goes beyond the hierarchy. It's not just your boss. It's also those who influence your boss: his or her friends, advisers, and confidants. It's those who have budgets and influential roles, those who are considered high potential for moving ahead in their careers, those who provide feedback in your reviews, and those who make decisions about hiring, new assignments, and promotions. Those with power may also not be whom you expect. It may be the college intern in your department whose uncle is a senior executive in the company or the admin who is the executive's trusted confidant. Even the squeaky wheel wields power. The people with power can make or break your reputation. Figure out who those people are and get to know them. Invite them to coffee. Understand their roles and what they're trying to accomplish. Offer to help.

- Build and carefully guard your reputation. This keeps coming up, doesn't it? Your reputation has everything to do with political clout and influence. Earn people's trust and respect by consistently delivering results, having integrity, and staying true to your word.

- Hold your cards close. Be careful whom you confide in. Assume even your most trusted confidant will share secrets with at least one other person.

- Consider all of the potential political ramifications.

In any situation, reflect on who will be affected by what you're saying and doing. Who's got the power? Maybe you need to ask. This is what landmines are about. They're dangerous because you don't see them. When Luanne started her job as a vice president at Juniper, she reached out to partners to understand their impressions of the company, which is crucial for building effective marketing programs. She was surprised to have her hand slapped by the head of sales for reaching out directly to customers without involving the sales team. While she strongly believed she didn't need permission to talk to partners, she recognized that she needed the sponsorship of the sales leader to be successful in her role so she agreed to play the game by his rules and keep him in the loop before calling on partners.

- Look for opportunities to be visible to those in power. Even small tasks present the opportunity to interact and be seen. For example, one of the young women on Alice's team, Regina, was a program manager supporting directors across Cisco. She went beyond the scope of program management and launched a fun and impactful campaign for professional development and recognition for the entire department. Consequently, she made a name for herself as a creative self-starter.

- Keep your emotions in check. We've talked a lot of about the importance of managing your emotions and, once again, it's critical for navigating politics. "The most important skill is the ability to master your emotions," according to Robert Greene. "An emotional response to a situation is the single biggest barrier to power, a mistake that will cost you a lot more than any other temporary satisfaction you may get from expressing your feelings. Emotions cloud reason, and if you cannot see the situation clearly, you cannot prepare for and respond to it with any degree of control."

This area has been the toughest for both of us to master in our careers. We wish someone had given us the rulebook for the power game when we were younger. Luanne had a boss who once told her she didn't capitalize enough on her power. She realized that in creating her daily To Do list, she had to think strategically about power. It's part of your day-to-day job. Figure out the game and get in it. Build your own political capital. Now is the perfect time to learn about power because it gets more complicated and the stakes are higher as you move ahead in your career.

Cathie Black, former chairman of Hearst Magazines, says "Power is something you can, and should, be able to develop for yourself—no matter where your position happens to be on the professional totem pole."

BLACK'S DEFINITIONS OF POWER

- Keeping your eye on the big picture. Don't get tangled in perceived personal slights; focus on suggestions for improving your company.

- Understanding what you can and cannot control. "In any office environment, there are many factors you can't control—the trickiest of which is often interpersonal. People get on each other's nerves, step on each other's toes, vie for each other's jobs, and, sometimes, at the other end of the spectrum, get inappropriately involved with each other. The only thing you can do is accept what you cannot change and work around it."

- Choosing your battles carefully. "You put yourself in a much more powerful position if you take the time to decide when to respond, and when to let something lie."

- Controlling the flow of information. "Don't tell people more than they've asked for. Keep a lid on it, and keep control of your information."

- Knowing your strengths and weaknesses. "Play up your strengths and make sure your team knows where you can add the most value."

- Not getting overly caught up in the idea of power. "Buying into the idea that you're personally powerful is the quickest way to lose perspective. Power might be a side effect of your success, but it shouldn't be the ultimate goal. If you seek power for its own sake, you'll succeed only in distancing yourself from your management, your team, and your goals. But if you do your job well, focus on your strengths, and work on your weaknesses, you'll naturally accrue power along the way. Keep a balanced perspective."

- Knowing you don't have to throw bombs. "True power is motivating a team and meeting your goals without having to crack the whip. It's having the confidence—both self-confidence and the confidence of your team—to make things happen without needing to browbeat."

- Knowing how to let things go. "No one wants to make a mistake, of course, but we all do. So the key is to move on quickly, and not wallow in self-defeating regret."

14

Manage Your Emotions at Work

THERE are plenty of reasons to get angry, frustrated, anxious, stressed, offended, and overwhelmed at work. Find ways to rise above negative emotions because what you're being measured on is getting the job done well with a positive attitude.

One of the young women we interviewed, Heather, a director of marketing in high tech, said her biggest "aha" as she transitioned from college to work was the pressure that comes from conflict.

You can't escape conflict. There are power struggles, competition, alliances, and different approaches and styles—a million situations that will cause conflict. We've found that many women will do whatever they can to avoid it (which creates a whole other set of problems). Rather than run from it, force yourself to understand and resolve it. Start by being self-reflective about a situation of conflict. Are you being emotional or taking things personally? Do you have all the information? There may be a bigger agenda in play. Get advice. Tap into your network and ask someone you trust for perspective. The goal is to get to resolution fairly quickly, then move on.

Another emotional challenge is working with difficult people. Both of us have worked with people who pushed our buttons. What we found is that we had to teach ourselves to make our interactions with those people transactional. What does that mean? Not getting hooked into their emotional game. Focus less on the person and more on the work: transactional activities. No gossip. No heated conversations. No games. Just focus on getting the job done.

If the difficult person is affecting the productivity of your work group and causing attrition, let your boss know. If your boss is the problem, let his or her boss know—but protect yourself by ensuring the negative impact is grounded in facts, not emotion and opinions.

For your own sanity, acknowledge what's going on. It can be helpful to write your feelings down or share them with a trusted friend. Give yourself a certain amount of time to agonize about the situation and then "change the track" in your head. Don't make it a mental loop that keeps you up at night. (We know this one's easier said than done.)

While we're on the topic of emotions, we'd like to say a few words about crying in the office.

The reality is you're spending many of your waking hours at work. It's totally normal there will be circumstances at work where you may want to cry. We're not talking about the tears that come with a personal loss or physical injury. We're not suggesting you be less than authentic at work. There are situations where it's okay to cry at work with someone you're comfortable with. We're talking about crying because you're exhausted, overwhelmed or frustrated, you've gotten tough feedback, or your feelings have been hurt. If you feel that emotion welling up at work, it's best to excuse yourself from the conversation gracefully. Have your cry in private. Then take a breath, have a sip of water, and put your game face on. The reason is that crying can be perceived as unprofessional and even manipulative. It puts people you work with in the awkward situation of having to comfort you. Our best advice is to avoid crying publicly.

Mastering your emotions affects how you're perceived as a business professional. "Getting smart about emotions at work is not some airy-fairy luxury," writes Anne Kreamer in *It's Always Personal: Navigating Emotion in the New Workplace.* "Emotion management is an essential skill set for success at work."

15
Take Control of Your Time

THERE'S one constant in life: everybody gets 24 hours in a day. H. Jackson Brown Jr. said it well: "Don't say you don't have enough time. You have exactly the same number of hours per day that were given to Helen Keller, Pasteur, Michelangelo, Mother Teresa, Leonardo da Vinci, Thomas Jefferson, and Albert Einstein."

Don't take the easy route, being passive and unconscious about your day. Those days add up—and, as we've learned in our 50s, time goes by surprisingly fast and you never get that time back. Be strategic in setting aside time to think, plan, and be creative.

If you want to have more impact, evaluate how you're spending your time. Start by looking at your calendar for the past month and ask yourself:

- How much time did you spend in reactive mode at work? Early in your career, you're expected to be responsive and follow through. You've got to do that well. Being promoted is about being proactive and going above and beyond.

- How much time did you spend working alone? Make sure you're connecting with new people and staying visibly in the mix. Network! You can't be successful working in a bubble.

- How much time did you spend with your boss? At the very least, initiate regular one-on-one meetings if your boss doesn't and ask for regular feedback on how you're doing. You could even ask your boss his or her opinion about how you're managing your time.

- Did you over-invest time and emotional energy with certain people? One of the rewarding parts of your career can be using your energy to mentor, coach, and guide people at work. Be strategic about how much emotional energy you spend and with whom. Avoid the work equivalent of the needy friend who leaves you feeling drained. You only get 24 hours in a day; don't give them away.

- Does where you're spending your time line up with your career goals and your brand?

Set aside time each week to plan how you're going to use your time. That could be Sunday night or 10 minutes with your chai latte on Monday morning. No phone, no distractions. Focus on yourself and be thoughtful about how you will prioritize your time for the upcoming week. Time management is important for every aspect of your life. We've found that if you proactively manage your time for all of your top priorities—including family, work, even your workouts—you're a happier, more productive person.

One executive that Luanne worked with started a routine in his 20s of blocking one hour each week to think. He would turn off all of his devices and just think. He said it has made a huge difference in his career and contributed to him becoming known for being proactive and coming up with new ideas.

We've found that a helpful method for prioritizing time is *The Rule of 10-10-10*, a decision-making guide created by Suzy Welch, author of the bestseller *10-10-10: A Life-Transforming Idea*. Ask yourself, what are the consequences of my decision in 10 minutes, 10 months, and 10 years? If the situation has lasting impact, it is important enough to be prioritized. This creates ownership on how you spend your time.

Speaking of making the most of your time, we know multitasking is today's reality. In 2014, *TIME Magazine* reported that people check their phone on average 110 times a day. Some people check as much as 900 times a day. When you're multitasking, you're in your own world. It's hard to have executive presence when you're multitasking.

Alexis, a young successful salesperson, cautions: "Don't multitask. Focus. Slow down to speed up. The power of full engagement really works."

Plus, you may be sending the wrong messages as you text and instant message in meetings. Do you ever see YouTube videos where people are presenting and texting on their phone at the same time? No. That's not compelling for an audience. Don't you get frustrated when you try to speak with someone who's multitasking? At work, it can be perceived as being unfocused, disrespectful, and passive aggressive. Leave your phone in your purse for important meetings.

Plus, there's an upside if you take a break from multitasking. Dr. Laura Ruby, who writes the blog *Stress, Life Balance & the Butterfly Effect,* found that even 15 minutes a day unconnected and device-free is linked to greater happiness, more success, and feeling more control over your time.

16

Invest in Yourself

INVESTING in yourself is a huge confidence builder. It takes discipline when there are so many demands on your time and energy, but it's worth it. And so are you! You can't be at the top of your game if you're physically run-down, one step behind on the knowledge and skills you need for work, or constantly stressed out about things like money. Of course, there will be times when you're on deadline and you've got to put in the hours. We're advocating giving yourself permission to set boundaries and prioritize time for self-renewal, which will make you a happier, more productive person.

We talked to young women across California, the Northeast, the Midwest, and the South and they all agreed one of their biggest challenges when working full-time was putting themselves first.

What's your self-investment plan?

It starts with your physical body. This is not about being skinny; it's about having energy and feeling powerful. You'll be able to concentrate and maintain a positive attitude if you eat well, get seven or eight hours of sleep a night, and get some form of physical exercise every day. If you get into the regular practice, it becomes part of your routine and doesn't feel like a "should" hanging over your head.

In terms of exercise, schedule the time on your calendar as if it were a meeting. What we've found is if you do your exercise in the morning before the insanity of the day, you're more likely to stick with it. It could be a run, a swim, a yoga class, anything physical. It will clear your mind, strengthen your body, and help you sleep. If working out truly isn't your thing, schedule time for something that relaxes you and brings you happiness, such as meditation, painting, or cooking.

Invest in your professional development. Most of the time, your boss will not be thinking about specific things you need to do to develop and grow. You've got the ball on this. When you have a one-on-one with your manager, go in prepared with a list of classes or opportunities for your professional development. Maybe you want to learn more about negotiation and influence or improve your PowerPoint skills. Many companies offer internal classes. Local universities offer courses and workshops. You can easily download books or take online courses through web sites such as Udacity, Coursera, and Skillshare. One of our favorite ideas is taking 20 minutes to watch a TED Talk. Twenty minutes a week adds up to almost 20 hours a year of learning something new.

Lastly, literally invest in yourself. We're not going to shake our fingers and tell you how to spend your money. But we are! You'll regret it when you're 50 if you haven't taken advantage of this tip. Whether you work for a company, a nonprofit, or the government, there will usually be some form of retirement savings plan. It's a pre-tax deduction, so it won't impact your paycheck as much you think. In a 2014 study of 3.5 million employees with 401k's, the average worker in his or her 20s reported saving 7.6% of his or her salary. If the average worker in her 20s, earning $50,000 a year, boosted her savings rate by just 1% (which is only $500) a year, her 401k balance would increase from an eventual $1.1 million to $1.2 million at age 65. Increase it by another 1%, and the account projected value increases to almost $1.3 million by retirement. That's a weekly lunch out you could sacrifice for another $100,000 to $200,000 for your retirement. Pack your lunch!

One book we recommend is Suze Orman's *Women & Money: Owning the Power to Control Your Destiny*. In her opening chapter she writes: "If we aren't powerful with money, we aren't powerful period. What is at stake here is not just money—it's far bigger. This is about a sense of who you are and what you deserve." She urges women to own taking the power of their financial destiny. This is why taking ownership of salary negotiations, as we discussed earlier in the book, is so important.

And let us tell you, it feels damn good to make money. Making your own income gives you choices. Go earn! (And don't forget to save!)

17

Champion Women

"There is a special place in hell for women who don't support each other."

—Madeleine Albright, former U. S. Secretary of State

WE'VE all heard the stats. Only 14.6% of executive officer and 16.9% of board of director seats at Fortune 500 companies were held by women in 2013, according to Catalyst.

Since women make up more than half of the management and professional workforce, according to Catalyst, we have the sheer muscle to push more women to the top if we support one another in taking risks and pursuing leadership opportunities.

In our experience, you'll work with more women who are supportive than aren't. Take Diane, who was a vice president of human resources at Cisco and a mentor, coach, and friend to both Alice and Luanne. She provided strategic advice to Alice on how to get promoted and how to handle difficult work situations. She also coached Luanne on operating as an executive when she was first promoted to vice president and was an advocate for the annual events Luanne hosted for hundreds of women in the company. Diane is a role model for achieving the balance of being a successful businesswoman with a warm Southern style.

Surround yourself with good women (and men!). Your female network can be a huge competitive advantage and can make you better. As we wrote this book, we tapped into our network of women for interviews, research, and expertise in publishing, editing, design, and marketing.

Make a conscious decision early in your career to be an advocate for other women. As you do, here are some questions to ask yourself and answer honestly:

- Am I gossiping, sabotaging, or undermining other women?

- Am I competitive with other women? We're not talking about being competitive for delivering business results and striving to win; that's a great quality at work. We're talking about personal competition at the expense of other women in your organization.

- Do I have issues with women in power? In any power structure, there's a coach and there are players. At game time, the coach calls the shots. Most men know to intuitively defer to the coach, even if they disagree with the play. Ask yourself, if your boss is a woman, do you support her as the coach? If she needs to be a better coach, can you provide feedback that will help her develop and grow?

- Am I connecting with other women? Are you networking and joining communities of women? Sheryl Sandberg's Lean In circles (leanincircles.org) for women are a good start.

- Am I mentoring and coaching other women? Even in your 20s, there are women who will benefit from your perspective, skills, and experience.

The bottom line is advocating for women is good for business. It's positive for your brand and creates a circle of goodwill around you. It also feels good to support your female colleagues. Don't be insecure; help other women. If women are good with each other, it puts other women and men at ease, which creates a more cooperative work environment.

We have a better chance of getting more women in future generations into top leadership positions if we support one another.

18
Build Your Confidence!

"Go confidently in the direction of your dreams! Live the life you've imagined." —Henry David Thoreau

CONFIDENCE is an area where many women struggle in their careers—all the way up to the CEO level. Joyce Roche, President and CEO of Girls, Inc. and author of *The Empress Has No Clothes: Conquering Self-Doubt to Embrace Success*, wrote in an essay published in *What I Know Now: Letters to My Younger Self*: "You're not an imposter. You're the genuine article. You have the brainpower. You have the ability. You don't have to work so hard and worry so much. You're going to do just fine."

Low self-confidence can be very damaging to your career. If you lack confidence, you will be tentative with your voice. You're unsure of yourself, so you are less likely to speak up at meetings. You're also less likely to put yourself out there for new opportunities and will feel undeserving of promotions. You hold yourself back.

There are a lot of theories to explain why this is true. But our interest is in giving you practical strategies that you can use in your day-to-day job to strengthen your confidence muscle. We are strong believers, and we've learned from personal experience, that you can "fake it until you make it."

We agree with Katty Kay and Claire Shipman, who wrote in the article "The Confidence Gap" in a 2014 *The Atlantic* article: "Confidence can be acquired."

These journalists interviewed Cameron Anderson, a psychologist who works in the business school at U.C. Berkeley, who said: "When people are confident, when they feel they are good at something, regardless of how good they actually are, they display a lot of confident nonverbal and verbal behavior. They have expansive body language, a lower vocal tone, and a tendency to speak up early and often in a calm, relaxed manner. They do a lot of things that make them look very confident in the eyes of others."

Our advice is to adjust your verbal and nonverbal behaviors to project self-confidence, and "owning" your confidence will follow.

Here's a checklist of five things you can do to boost your confidence every day.

1. Get inside your head. Put yourself in a confident mindset by thinking of yourself in positive terms. Pull out your journal and write down your business strengths (e.g., strong negotiator, team player, critical thinker). Write them on an index card and put them in a place where you'll see them daily, such as your makeup mirror, car dashboard, or next to your coffee pot. Or put them in *Notes* on your phone so

you can remind yourself digitally each day. The sad reality is 77% of self-talk is negative, according to leadership expert and author John Maxwell. Change the conversation in your head. Confidence means "with trust"—so learn to trust your skills, ideas, and intuition.

2. Select strong language. We mentioned this earlier in the Communications section. Confident people use powerful words; opt for words like "leading," "managing" and "creating." Drop fillers and non-words, such as "um," "really" and "you know." They detract from confidence.

3. Use your voice as a tool to project confidence and self-respect. Speak slowly. Enunciate your words. Work with your voice volume, tone, and pace to convey messages of self-assurance. You want to sound calm and in control, not frantic and anxious.

4. Try power poses. Amy Cuddy, a social psychologist at the Harvard Business School, has found that just as the alpha dog projects dominance and power by puffing up his chest, making grand gestures, and taking up physical space, the process also works in reverse. We know this may feel weird, but her research shows that if you puff up your chest, use grand gestures, and take up physical space for a matter of two minutes, your body chemistry changes—and you begin to feel powerful and confident!

5. Set yourself up for success. Two words: prepare and practice.

The result of tweaking your behaviors is you'll feel more confident. As you feel more confident, you'll raise your hand, take more risks, and attract more opportunities. Confidence begets more confidence. Before you know it, you've got a strong confidence muscle. Nurturing your self-confidence has to become part of your daily ritual. Apply mascara; apply these tips. Repeat!

MY BUSINESS STRENGTHS AND REASONS TO BE CONFIDENT

19
Develop Perspective

PERSPECTIVE is a valuable leadership skill, and one you can begin developing now. It's a given you must do your job well. That will earn a good performance review. But that's not enough to get ahead. Having a broader perspective than your job can help you leapfrog in your career.

If you want to stand out and demonstrate business savvy, understand the bigger picture and bring that understanding to your day-to-day job. Let us give you some examples. If your boss is working on a big presentation, share relevant research that may help his or her talk. If your department is looking at reorganizing, provide benchmarking on how similar departments at other companies are organized. If you're presenting a new idea or initiative, share that idea with a few people first and gain consensus to make sure you don't have a blind spot.

The way you become adept at getting perspective is taking a moment to step back to grasp the bigger picture and constantly seeking out additional data in order to make intelligent decisions.

Jessica, CEO of a Silicon Valley technology company, said in hiring employees she looks for people "who can help the company build valuable relationships and who can connect the dots and solve problems. Every employee should see themselves as a cost center and figure out what he or she needs to do to increase company revenue." She shared the story of a young woman in her company who doesn't bring new ideas forward. "She doesn't see the bigger picture of how her department drives revenue for the business."

Wendy, a C-level executive, agrees. "If you want to have perspective, understand sales. How does the company make money, and what can you do in your role to help the process of making more money for your company?"

Having perspective also relates to your brand. Do you want to be a subject matter expert in a certain area? If so, keep current with the latest trends and developments. Become knowledgeable on that topic and apply new ideas to your work. Have a point of view, and back it up with data.

Last thought! Perspective is also about understanding that your career is a journey that will span decades. You will have many roles and many bosses. If you're in a tough spot, try to remember it's just one chapter in your career. We've found that, even though it's trite, the toughest times are often the greatest learning experiences. If you're in a good situation, enjoy it! It's both the good situations and the bad that will add to your wisdom and enrich your sense of perspective, which can become a huge competitive advantage in your career. The good news is that you are gaining perspective every day!

HOW MUCH PERSPECTIVE DO YOU HAVE?

- What are the vision, mission, and goals for your organization or company?
- Does your company have a Corporate Overview or

other messaging documents? (They're typically found on the company website) Have you read them?

- What products and services does your company offer?

- How does your company make money? (Direct and/ or indirect channels?)

- What's your company's selling process? Have you ever seen a sales pitch?

- Have you spent any time with a sales rep and/or customers? What challenges do they face?

- Are you familiar with departments outside of your own? Have you set up informational interviews or shadowed a colleague to have a better understanding of how other departments work?

- What are other departments looking for from your team to help the company be more successful?

- Do you know your company calendar of events? When are the big events, such as the annual sales meeting or quarterly earnings call?

- If you work for a publicly traded company, do you know what your company announced in its most recent earnings?

- Who are your company's top competitors?

- What are the trends in your industry?

- Are you following your company and competitors in the news and on social media? What's being said?

- What are the top three stories in the news this week?

20

Define Your Own Success

YOUR twenties are about laying the foundation for your career and your life.

"Your twenties matter," writes Meg Jay in her book, *The Defining Decade: Why Your Twenties Matter—and How To Make the Most of Them Now.* "Eighty percent of life's most defining moments take place by age thirty-five. Two-thirds of lifetime wage growth happens in the first ten years of your career. More than half of us are married, or dating, or living with our future partner by age thirty. Personality changes more during our twenties than at any time before or after. The brain caps off its last growth spurt in the twenties."

Jay advises people in their twenties to not spend too much time navel-gazing but to go out there and do! By gaining skills and experiences and making new connections, you build your "identity capital."

"Identity capital is our collection of personal assets," she explains. "It is the repertoire of individual resources that we assemble over time. These are the investments we make in ourselves, the things we do well enough, or long enough, that they become a part of who we are. Some identity goes on a resume, such as degrees, jobs, test scores and clubs. Other identity capital is more personal, such as how we speak, where we are from, how we solve problems, how we look. Identity capital is how build ourselves—bit by bit, over time. Most important, identity capital is what we bring to the adult marketplace. It is the currency we use to metaphorically purchase jobs and relationships and other things we want."

You begin building this foundation for your career in your twenties by learning, experimenting, and taking risks. As one of Jay's clients put it: "You can't pull some great career out of a hat in your thirties. You've got to start in your twenties."

In our twenties, we were open and tried new things.

Luanne's first job was as a marketing coordinator at First Deposit Corporation; she was hired after doing a college internship. She took a contracting stint at Apple, was recruited by HP, and then was recruited by 3Com Corp.—all in marketing roles.

Alice's first job after getting her master's in journalism was as a reporter covering the political beat. She discovered she hated the adversarial role of covering politics and moved to a small public relations firm. She worked for a brilliant man, but the company was out of business within a year and a half. Then a friend connected her with a corporate communications role at AT&T, which ultimately led to a job transfer from San Francisco to Manhattan at 29.

We experienced many different companies, bosses, and roles. Your twenties are the time to get exposure to new opportunities, new people, and new jobs!

Your idea of career success will change depending on what's going on in your life. We want to point out that you can have a stimulating career no matter what life phase you're moving through.

For example, Luanne started a family at 30 as she was managing a team of seven. The practical reality was she had to work, but she scaled it back to four days a week. Success at that time in her life was meaningful work and flexibility. When her youngest was in first grade, she went back full time. In her 40s, she focused on career. She came to terms with the struggle of being a working mom because she liked the buzz of the business world and making money, and loved being a mom. One of her strategies that she learned from the late Ann Richards, former governor of Texas, for integrating work and life was bringing her daughter, Lauren, on business trips. This also gave her daughter exposure and appreciation for her mom's career.

Alice's definition of success changed after breast cancer in 2010. Her life priorities shifted and success was about flexibility and focusing on work she loved: writing, coaching, and consulting. While recovering from surgery, she wrote down what success looked like for her, laminated the list, and put it on the mirror in her master bathroom so she'd see it every day. Shortly soon after, she started her own consulting practice and focused on work she enjoyed.

Success is very personal. Think about what success looks like to you—and don't get swayed by TV, social media, and/or friends. It's easy to think everyone else is having the perfect life. They're posting photos from their vacations, the parties they're attending, and all their good news. Don't let that get in your head and affect your own vision of success. Stop comparing! Only you know what will feel like success for you.

Keep in mind, you're not going to feel like Wonder Woman every day. Nor should you. It's normal to have doubts and insecurities. If you're taking risks and pushing yourself, you will fail and make mistakes. Making mistakes and being nervous are part of growth. Success is achieved with little steps over time. Although we wrote this book for women in their twenties, these tips are a "go to" list for your entire career. Evolving your brand, taking risks, building your network never ends! We believe in you and hope the advice we've given you can help you can achieve great things in your life. You deserve it. You're worth it. Now, go for it!

All our best,

Celine & Luanne

References

SET CAREER GOALS
- Sara Blakely, "Improving her assets," by Beth Silcox, *SUCCESS Magazine*, March 29, 2009.
- Sheryl Sandberg, COO, Facebook. "The Geek's Guide to the Writing Life: Sheryl Sandberg's Lean In and Lessons for Writers," by Stephanie Vanderslice, *Huffington Post*, April 12, 2013.

CREATE A PERSONAL BRAND
- Tom Peters, *Fast Company*, 1997. Used by permission of Tom Peters. See tompeters.com for additional information.
- Sylvia Ann Hewlett, *Executive Presence: The Missing Link Between Merit and Success*. First edition. Copyright © 2014 by Sylvia Ann Hewlett. HarperCollins Publishers, New York.
- William Arruda and Kirsten Dixson, *Career Distinction: Stand Out by Building Your Brand*. Copyright © 2007 by William Arruda and Kirsten Dixson. Published by John Wiley & Sons, Inc., Hoboken, New Jersey.
- William Arruda and Deb Dib. *Ditch, Dare, Do: 3D Personal Branding for Executives*. First edition. Copyright © 2012 by William Arruda and Deb Dib. Published by TradesMark Press International, New York.

MANAGE YOUR ONLINE PRESENCE
- Gary Vaynerchuk, *Jab, Jab, Jab, Right Hook: How to Tell Your Story in a Noisy Social World*. First Edition, Copyright © 2013, Harper Collins, New York, New York
- Katherine Schwarzenegger, *I Just Graduated...Now What?* First edition. Copyright © by Katherine Schwarzenegger. Published by Crown Archetype, an imprint of the Crown Publishing Group, a division of Random House LLC, a Penguin Random House Company, New York.

GROW YOUR PROFESSIONAL NETWORK

- Debra Fine. *The Fine Art of Small Talk: How to Start a Conversation, Keep It Going, Build Networking Skills— and Leave a Positive Impression!* First Edition. Copyright © 2005. Hyperion Books, New York, NY.

- Jacqueline Whitmore, "Break the Ice: 8 Networking Tips for Introverts." Entrepreneur.com, May 12, 2014.

- Susan Cain. *Quiet: The Power of Introverts in a World That Can't Stop Talking.* Copyright © 2012, 2013 by Susan Cain. First paperback edition. Published by Broadway Books, an imprint of the Crown Publishing Company, a division of Random House, Inc., New York.

- "The Strength of Weak Ties," Mark S. Granovetter. *American Journal of Sociology*, Volume 78, Issue 6 (May 1973), 1360-1380. © 1973 University of Chicago Press.

- Malcolm Gladwell, *The Tipping Point: How Little Things Can Make a Big Difference*, First Edition. Copyright © 2002, 2002. Little, Brown and Company; New York, NY.

SEEK OUT MENTORS AND ATTRACT SPONSORS

- Ora Shtull. *The Glass Elevator: A Guide to Leadership Presence for Women on the Rise.* Copyright © 2012 Ora Shtull. Published by 85 Broads, Greenwich, Connecticut.

- Keith Ferrazzi, *Never Eat Alone and Other Secrets to Success, One Relationship at a Time.* First Edition. Copyright © 2005. Doubleday Random House; New York, NY.

NEGOTIATE EVERYTHING; "ASKING" IS A BUSINESS SKILL

- Linda Babcock. *Women Don't Ask: Negotiation and the Gender Divide.* Second Edition. Copyright © 2008. Piatkus Books; London, Great Britain.

- Margaret Neale. "Why Women Must Ask (the right way): Negotiation Advice from Stanford's Margaret A. Neale." Forbes.com. June 17, 2013.

PRACTICE GOOD BUSINESS ETIQUETTE

- Peggy Post & Peter Post, *The Etiquette Advantage in Business: Personal Skills for Professional Success.* Second edition. Copyright © 2005 by the Emily Post Institute, Inc. HarperCollins Publishers, Inc., New York.

- Tim Sackett, President of HRU Technical Resources, *11 Rules for Hugging at Work*, LinkedIn: https://www.linkedin.com/pulse/20140227203309-5926874-11-rules-for-hugging-at-work

BE A ROCK STAR COMMUNICATOR

- 2014 Corporate Recruiters Survey. Graduate Management Admission Council in partnership with MBA Career Services & Employer Alliance. Copyright © 2014 Graduate Admission Council (GMAC)

- Timothy Koegel, *The Exceptional Presenter: A Proven Formula to Open Up! And Own the Room.* Copyright © Timothy J. Koegel. Published by Greenleaf Book Group Press, Austin, Texas.

- Mary Brienza. As quoted in *The Glass Elevator: A Guide to Leadership Presence for Women on the Rise.* Copyright © 2012 Ora Shtull. Published by 85 Broads, Greenwich, Connecticut.

- Malcolm Gladwell, *Blink: The Power of Thinking Without Thinking.* First Edition. Copyright © 2005. Little Brown and Company, New York, NY.

- Matt Abrahams, *Speaking Up Without Freaking Out: 35 Techniques for Confident, Calm, and Competent Presenting.* Copyright © 2012, 2010 by Matt Abrahams. Kendall Hunt Publishing Company, Dubuque, Iowa.

STAND OUT; BE VISIBLE

- "Managing Yourself: Women, Find Your Voice." By Kathryn Heath, Jill Flynn, and Mary Davis Holt. 2012 Harvard Business Review. http://hbr.org/2014/06/women-find-your-voice/ar/pr

RECOVER WELL FROM DISAPPOINTMENTS AND MISTAKES

- Michael Jordan. www.brainyquote.com

- Marie Forleo. www.marieforleo.com

BE POLITICALLY SMART

- Dr. Lois Frankel, *Nice Girls Don't Get the Corner Office: 101 Unconscious Mistakes Women Make that Sabotage Their Careers.* First Revised Edition. Copyright © 2014. Grand Central Publishing; New York, NY.

- "Four Executives on Succeeding in Business as a Woman," By Adam Bryant, Corner Office, *The New York Times*. October 12, 2013. http://www.nytimes.com/interactive/2013/10/13/business/women-corner-office.html
- Robert Greene, *The 48 Laws of Power*. Copyright © Joost Elffers and Robert Greene, 1998. Published by Penguin Group, New York.
- Jeffrey Pfeffer, *Power: Why Some People Have It—And Others Don't*. First edition. Copyright © 2010 by Jeffrey Pfeffer. Published by HarperCollins Publishers, New York.
- Cathie Black. *Basic Black: The Essential Guide for Getting Ahead at Work (and in Life)*. Copyright © 2007 by Cathleen P. Black. Published by Three Rivers Press, an imprint of the Crown Publishing Group, a division of Random House, New York.

MANAGE YOUR EMOTIONS AT WORK

- Anne Kreamer. *It's Always Personal: Navigating Emotion in the Workplace*. First Edition. Copyright © 2011, 2012 by Bedoozled Inc.Random House; New York, NY.

TAKE CONTROL OF YOUR TIME

- "The Rule of 10-10-10," a guide to decision making, by Suzy Welch. September 2006 issue of *O, The Oprah Magazine*. http://www.oprah.com/spirit/Suzy-Welchs-Rule-10-10-10-Decision-Making-Guide/1?print=1
- "Study Shows We Unlock Our Phones a LOT Each Day," by Doug Aamoth, October 8, 2013, *TIME Magazine*. Article quotes study released by app maker Locket. http://techland.time.com/2013/10/08/study-says-we-unlock-our-phones-a-lot-each-day/print
- Dr. Laura Ruby, Stress, Life Balance & the Butterfly Effect www.drlauraruby.com

INVEST IN YOURSELF

- "Are You Saving Enough for Retirement?" by Walter Updegrave, *The Wall Street Journal*. July 31, 2014. http://online.wsj.com/articles/are-you-saving-enough-for-retirement-140683169
- Suzy Orman, *Women & Money: Owning the Power to Control Your Destiny*. Copyright © 2007, 2010 by Suze Orman, a Trustee of the Suze Orman Revocable Trust.

Published by Spiegel & Grau, an imprint of The Random House Publishing Group, a division of Random House, Inc., New York.

CHAMPION WOMEN
- Madeleine Albright. www.goodreads.com
- 2013 Catalyst Census reports: Fortune 500 Women Board Directors and Fortune 500 Women Executive and Top Wage Earners. www.catalyst.org
- Lean In Circles. "Circles are small peer groups that meet regularly to learn and share together. Studies show we achieve more in groups than we do as individuals. A Circle can be a monthly roundtable at your house, a regular brown-bag lunch or even a virtual meet-up." Leanincircles.org

BUILD YOUR CONFIDENCE!
- *What I Know Now: Letters to My Younger Self*, edited by Ellyn Spragins. Copyright © 2006 by Ellyn Spragins. Published by Broadway Books, an imprint of The Doubleday Broadway Publishing Group, a division of Random House, Inc., New York.
- "Closing the Confidence Gap. Evidence shows that women are less self-assured than men—and that to succeed, confidence matters as much as competence. Here's why, and what to do about it," by Katty Kay and Claire Shipman. *The Atlantic*. April 14, 2014. http://www.theatlantic.com/features/archive/2014/04/the-confidence-gap/359815/
- John Maxwell, *The 15 Invaluable Laws of Growth; Live them and reach your potential*. First Edition, Copyright © 2012, Hachette Book Group, New York, NY.

DEFINE YOUR OWN SUCCESS
- Meg Jay, *The Defining Decade: Why Your Twenties Matter and How To Make the Most of Them Now*. First trade edition: April 2013. Copyright © 2012 by Meg Jay. Published by Hachette Book Group, an imprint of Grand Central Publishing, New York.

CPSIA information can be obtained at www.ICGtesting.com
Printed in the USA
LVOW05s1738030215

425458LV00002B/3/P